# HISTORY PRACTICE EXERCISES 13+

## Gavin Hannah and Paul Spencer

www.galorepark.co.uk

Published by ISEB Publications, an imprint of Galore Park
19/21 Sayers Lane, Tenterden, Kent TN30 6BW
www.galorepark.co.uk



Design and typography by Typetechnique
Printed by Replika Press Pvt. Ltd, India

ISBN: 978 0903627 77 1



First published 2009, reprinted 2010, 2011

Details of other ISEB publications, examination papers and Galore Park publications are available at www.galorepark.co.uk

The publishers are grateful for permission to use the photographs as follows: Cover image: Ms 22495 fol.287 Embarkation for abroad, from Le Roman de Godefroi de Bouillon, 1337 (vellum) by French School, (14th century) Bibliotheque Nationale, Paris, France/Giraudon/The Bridgeman Art Library Nationality/copyright status: French/out of copyright, p3 The London Art Archive/Alamy, p7 Look and Learnn/Bridgeman Art Library, p9 Mary Evans Picture Library, p11 Mary Evans Picture Library/Alamy, p13 Look and Learn/Bridgeman Art Library, p15 Bridgeman Art Library, p17 Look and Learn/Bridgeman Art Library, p19 British Library/akg-images, p23 National Archives, p25 Bridgeman Art Library, p27 Roger-Viollet, Paris/Bridgeman Art Library, p29 The London Art Archive/Alamym p31 City of London Libraries and Guildhall Art Gallery/Heritage Images, p33 Walker Art Gallery, National Museums Liverpool/Bridgeman Art Library, p35 Mary Evans Picture Library/Alamy, p36 Classic Image/Alamy, p39 Bridgeman Art Library, p41 The Print Collector /Alamy, p43 Mary Evans Picture Library/Alamy, p47 Fotomas/TopFoto, p49 Mary Evans Picture Library/Alamy, p51 The Print Collector/Heritage Images, p53 Museum of London, UK/Bridgeman Art Library, p55 HIP/Photo Scala, Florence, p57 Classic Image/Alamy, p59 Mary Evans Picture Library/Alamy, p61 Trade Union Congress/Tolpuddle Martyrs Museum Memorial Trust, p63 Library of Congress, Washington D.C./Bridgeman Art Library, p65 Punch/Zooid Pictures.

# Contents

**Essay Questions**

# Introduction

*History Practice Exercises 13+* is a book of sample Common Entrance-style questions based closely on the ISEB syllabus for all three periods, from 1066 to 1900. It offers a range of exciting and lively material and we hope you enjoy using it.

The Essay Questions are based on the major themes from the Common Entrance syllabus, while the Evidence Questions cover all the required topics. The same skills: comprehension; comparison; an assessment of the utility and reliability of material based on provenance are required for all history, so don't hesitate to use practice questions on periods which you are not studying for Common Entrance. New topics often bring a fresh sense of excitement and using unfamiliar material is a great way to highlight the underlying skills you are learning.

## Timing

Practise writing Evidence Questions allowing yourself **20 minutes**, which is the time suggested by the setters.

Essays should be completed within **35 minutes**.

If you are someone entitled to extra time, use it as you have been advised.

## Evidence Questions

Keep the first two answers short (watch the mark scheme). Use the words of the questions to help you make up your answers. In **Question 3**, be clear in your mind what Source C is saying, only then will you be able to compare it with the others. Do not forget to mention **differences** as well as **similarities**.

For **Question 4**, offer reasoned discussion and analysis based on the sources. Look fully at **all** sources, do not miss any out. Be critical, consider the provenance (**NOP: Nature, Origin, Purpose**) of each source. Do not be frightened to make a judgement on which source you believe to be the most useful. There is no right answer, but examiners like to see evidence of thinking.

## Essays

Be relevant. Keep a sense of focus. Produce **a question-led response**. Appreciate the difference between **Topic Knowledge** and **Question Knowledge**. Topic Knowledge means everything you have been taught about a topic, such as Medieval Monasteries or Robert Walpole. Question Knowledge means only the knowledge necessary to answer a particular question on the topic.

Make a **plan** to get a good structure. Include an **Introduction** and a **Conclusion** with reference to the essay title. Between these, there should be a series of **linked paragraphs** each making a particular point. Focus on the key facts. Distinguish between the two parts of the essay. Accurate narrative is required in the 'Describe' bit. Give clear reasons and judgements in the 'Explain why' bit. Note the different technique needed for the two different parts.

Above everything else, enjoy what you write and let that sparkle come through in your script. After all, you have chosen to tackle that particular essay. Good luck!

Gavin Hannah
Oxford
Spring 2009

## A note on syllabus changes

Following the publication of this book, a minor syllabus change means that, from Spring 2010, Religion will no longer be examined in the Section C (1750–1900) essay questions. However, as this book is designed to give pupils practice in answering a range of questions, the few Religion questions included in Section C should not be ignored, as they still provide practice in answering essay questions. Social Reform questions remain relevant, but as part of Social and Economic History instead of Religion and Social Reform. For more details on the history syllabus visit the Independent Schools Examinations Board (ISEB) website, www.iseb.co.uk.

Please also note that from Spring 2010 the date ranges will have changed to 1066–1485 and 1485–1750 and this change is reflected in this book. Both the old and new versions of the syllabus are available on the ISEB website.

# Evidence Questions

## A. Medieval Realms: Britain 1066–1485

# The First Crusade

***Read the introduction and the sources and then answer all the questions. You must refer to the sources in ALL your answers.***

*In 1095, at the Council of Clermont, Pope Urban II announced the launch of the first crusade. The aim was to capture Jerusalem from the Muslims and to recover the Holy Land in the name of Christianity. The following sources give information about the taking of Jerusalem in 1099 and the massacre of the inhabitants.*

1. Look at **Source A**. How did the Crusaders climb into Jerusalem? (2)
2. Look at **Source B**. What two reasons does the writer provide which explain why the slaughter was so great? (3)
3. Look carefully at **Source C**. How far does this source support the information given in Sources **A** and **B**? (7)
4. Look at **ALL** the sources. Which do you think offers the most useful evidence concerning the massacre at Jerusalem? (8)

**SOURCE A**: an extract, from the modern textbook *The Assault on Jerusalem* by S. Runciman, describing the attack on Jerusalem in 1099.

Once a section of the wall was captured, scaling ladders enabled many of the assailants [attackers] to climb into the city … The Crusaders, maddened by so great a victory after so much suffering, rushed through the streets and into the houses and mosques, killing all that they met, men, women and children alike.

**SOURCE B**: an extract from William of Tyre, a 12th century writer who described the fall of Jerusalem.

The valiant Godfrey of Bouillon, the knights and other men-at-arms who were with him, descended from the walls, all armed, into the town. They went together through the streets with their swords in their hands. All them that they met, they slew and smote [cut] down, unarmed men, women and children, sparing none … They slew so many in the street that there were heaps of dead bodies … The foot-soldiers went to other parts of the town holding in their hands great poleaxes and other weapons, slaying all the Turks they could find. For they [the Turks] were people that our men had the greatest hatred for and so would gladly put them to death.

**SOURCE C**: a 19th century painting, by Emile Signol, showing the final capture of Jerusalem by the crusaders on 15th July 1099.

# Matilda and Stephen

***Read the introduction and the sources and then answer all the questions. You must refer to the sources in ALL your answers.***

*Henry I named his daughter, Matilda, as his successor. However, on Henry's death in 1135, Stephen slipped across the Channel and claimed the throne. Matilda defended her rights. This led to a period of strife and chaos, during which men said that 'Christ and his angels slept'. The following sources all provide evidence about this civil war, which lasted until 1154.*

1. Look at **Source A**. Give one reason why Geoffrey was not able to beat King Stephen in 1137. (2)
2. Look at **Source B**. Give two reasons why Stephen was able to get enough backing to make himself king. (3)
3. Look at **Source C**. How does it help you to understand better Sources **A** and **B**? (7)
4. Look at **ALL** the sources. Which source do you think would be the most useful evidence of why the civil war between Stephen and Matilda started? (8)

**SOURCE A**: an extract, from Henry of Huntingdon's chronicle *Historia Anglorum* ('History of the English'), describing events in 1137. The chronicle was finished in 1154.

Geoffrey, Count of Anjou, was King Stephen's mortal enemy, for he had married King Henry's daughter Matilda, who … had received oaths of fealty [loyalty] for the kingdom of England, so that she and her husband laid claim to the crown. But … at present he could not make headway against King Stephen, on account of his numerous forces and of the great amount of money Stephen had found in the treasury of the late King Henry…

**SOURCE B**: an extract, from the modern history book *Norman Britain* by Henry Loyn and Alan Sorrell, describing the conflict between Matilda and Stephen.

The problem of succession was difficult. Henry finally persuaded the barons to recognise his daughter, Matilda, as heir, but she married Geoffrey Plantagenet, heir to the Count of Anjou, regarded by many Normans as their arch-enemy. Henry had heaped favours and lands on Matilda's cousin, Stephen of Blois, who was popular for his generosity … amongst the Norman barons. Henry died in 1135 and Stephen, acting quickly, had himself … crowned king. As grandson to the Conqueror he gained the support of many; as a man he gained the support of more who feared the rule of a woman.

**SOURCE C**: the family tree of the kings of England from 1066 to 1189, showing how the leading royals were related.

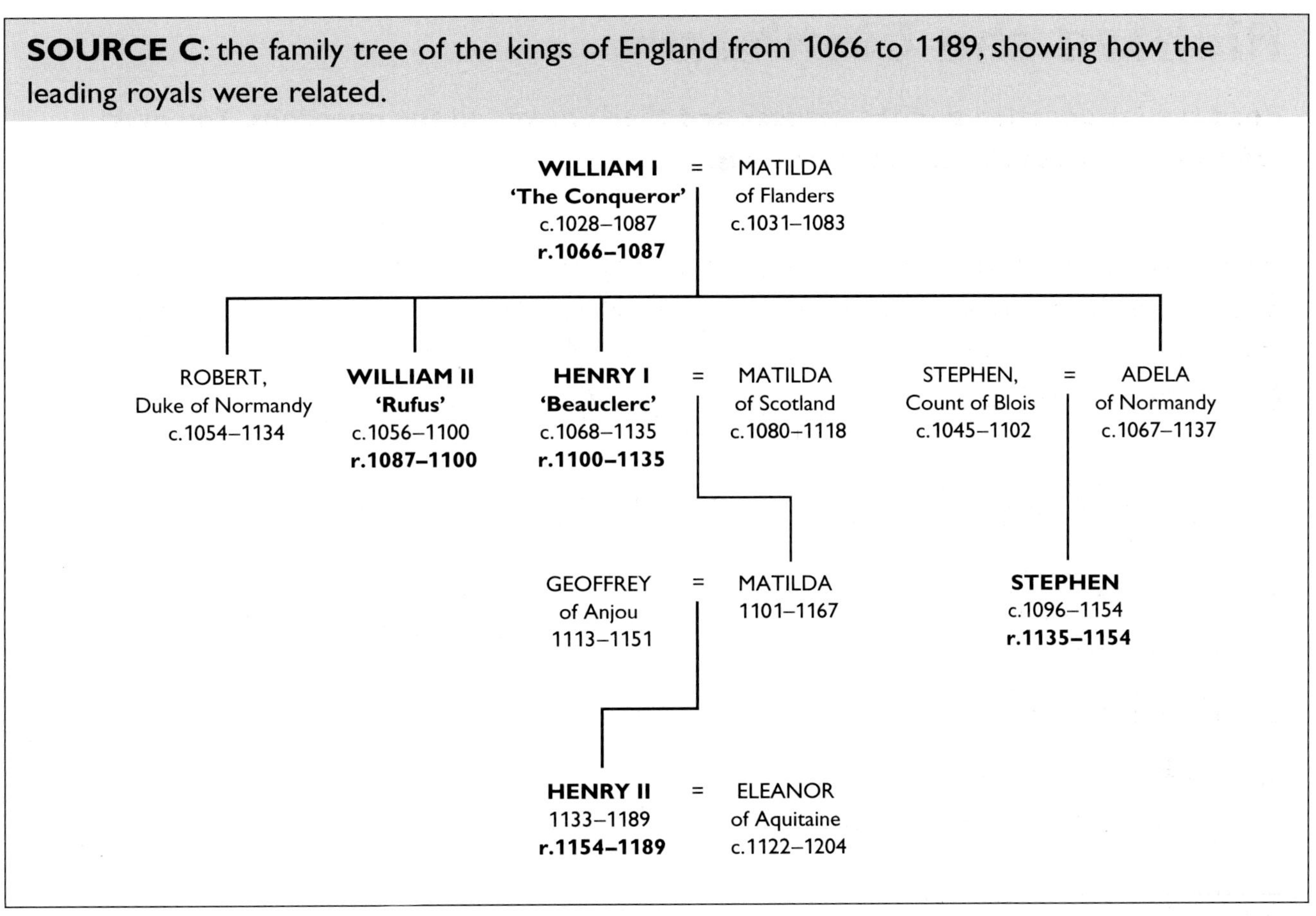

# Richard the Lionheart

***Read the introduction and the sources and then answer all the questions. You must refer to the sources in ALL your answers.***

*In 1190, Richard the Lionheart took the cross and set off from France to join the Third Crusade. The following sources give information about his achievements and his skills as a soldier.*

1. Look at **Source A**. Describe one of Richard's greatest achievements. (2)
2. Look at **Source B**. Give two ways in which Geoffrey de Vinsauf suggests that Richard the Lionheart inspired his men. (3)
3. Look carefully at **Source C**. How far does this source support the information given in Sources **A** and **B** concerning Richard's qualities as a warrior? (7)
4. Look at **ALL** the sources. Which do you think offers the most useful evidence concerning Richard's greatness on the battlefield? (8)

**SOURCE A**: an extract, from the modern textbook *The Three Richards* by N. Saul, describing some of the qualities of Richard I.

Richard the Lionheart's career was the stuff of which legends are made. He was one of the most inspirational rulers of his day. As a warrior he was more than a match for the renowned [famous] Saladin. He conquered a whole kingdom [Cyprus] in a matter of weeks. In the Holy Land, his siegecraft at Acre drew the admiration of the other crusading commanders. His achievements in politics and war were larger than life.

**SOURCE B**: an extract from Geoffrey de Vinsauf, a 12th century author, writing about Richard I at the Siege of Acre in 1191.

King Richard was not yet fully recovered from his sickness. Nevertheless, anxious for action, and intent upon taking the city [Acre], he made arrangements that his men should assault the city ... For this purpose, he caused to be made a hurdle. The king intended to use this for crossing over the trench outside the city. Under it he placed his most experienced arbalesters [crossbowmen], and caused himself to be carried there on a silken bed, to honour the Saracens with his presence, and to encourage his men to fight. From it, using his arbalest, in which he was skilled, he slew many with darts and arrows.

**SOURCE C**: a 20th century painting, by Peter Jackson of Richard the Lionheart fighting in the Third Crusade.

# King John

***Read the introduction and the sources and then answer all the questions. You must refer to the sources in ALL your answers.***

*King John had a troubled reign. In 1204 he lost Normandy and, soon afterwards, the rest of his French lands. He upset the Church and the Pope. He clashed with his barons who forced him to agree to* Magna Carta *in 1215. The following sources give information about King John as ruler.*

1. Look at **Source A**. Give one reason why King John sent messengers to his barons. (2)
2. Look at **Source B**. Describe two ways in which this author suggests that John was a good ruler. (3)
3. Look carefully at **Source C**. With which other source, **A** or **B**, does it most agree concerning John's abilities as a king? (7)
4. Look at **ALL** the sources. Which do you think offers the least useful evidence concerning John as a ruler? (8)

**SOURCE A**: an extract from the chronicle of Roger of Wendover, a monk of St Albans, writing soon after the events he describes.

King John saw that he was deserted by almost all, and was much alarmed in case the barons should attack his castles. He sent messengers to them and told them that for the sake of the peace and honour of his kingdom, he would willingly grant them the laws and liberties they required. He also sent word to appoint a fitting day and place to meet to carry out all these matters. The barons, in their great joy, chose the fifteenth of June for the king to join them at a field lying between Staines and Windsor.

**SOURCE B**: an extract, from modern historian V. H. Galbraith's textbook *Kings and Chroniclers*, commenting on John as a ruler.

Historians have been increasingly driven, however unwillingly, to recognise the great abilities of King John … He was loyally served till death by great ministers. His reform of the coinage, his development of trade and of the navy and defence, form a series of positive achievements which he handed on to his successors.

**SOURCE C**: a 19th century illustration of King John signing *Magna Carta* at Runnymede on 15th June 1215.

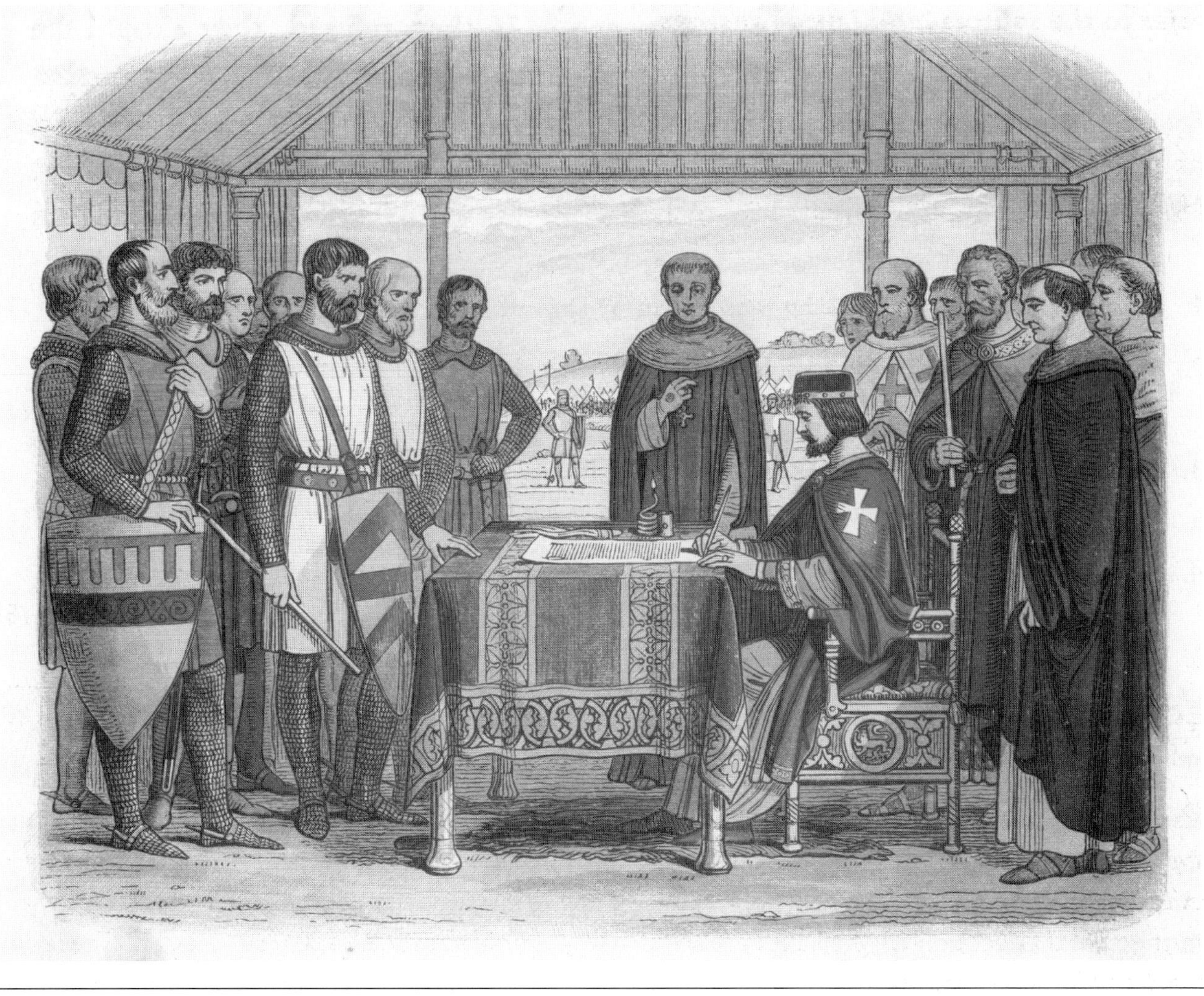

# Edward I, Wales and Scotland

***Read the introduction and the sources and then answer all the questions. You must refer to the sources in ALL your answers.***

*Edward I had a dream of uniting all the parts of Britain with himself as overlord. As part of this mission he made war on both Wales and Scotland. The following sources give information about Edward's military dealings with Scotland and, in particular, his treatment of the Scottish patriot, William Wallace.*

1. Look at **Source A**. Describe one way in which Edward I tried to beat the Scots. (2)
2. Look at **Source B**. Explain two methods by which this author shows his hatred of Wallace. (3)
3. Look carefully at **Source C**. How far does it support the evidence given in Sources **A** and **B** concerning the execution of William Wallace? (7)
4. Look at **ALL** the sources. Which do you think offers the most useful evidence concerning Edward I's policy towards the Scots? (8)

**SOURCE A**: the modern historian M. Prestwich, in *Plantagenet England 1225–1360*, comments on Edward I's attacks on Scotland.

Edward I led massive campaigns north in 1298, 1300, 1301 and 1303, pouring men and money into the war on a scale the Scots could not possibly match. The king's strategy of using overwhelming force worked ... The reality of Edward's attitude towards the Scots was shown in the brutal execution of Wallace in 1305.

**SOURCE B**: an extract from a 14th century English writer describing the execution of William Wallace.

William Wallace, a robber given to arson [setting fire to the property of other people] and homicide, more hardened in cruelty than King Herod ... was condemned to a most cruel but justly deserved death. He was drawn through the streets of London until he reached the gallows of unusual height. There he was suspended but taken down while still alive. His bowels were torn out and burned in a fire. His head was then cut off and his body divided into four parts. Behold the end of a merciless man, who himself perished without mercy.

**SOURCE C**: a modern illustration of William Wallace being dragged to his execution in 1305.

# Edward II and Scotland

***Read the introduction and the sources and then answer all the questions. You must refer to the sources in ALL your answers.***

*Edward II faced problems in Scotland, where Robert Bruce was trying to drive out the English. Bruce made devastating raids deep into northern England. He then threatened Stirling Castle, one of the last English strongholds. Edward II raised a massive force, marched north, and met Bruce at Bannockburn. The following sources all provide evidence about this great battle, which took place on 24th June 1314.*

1. Look at **Source A**. According to the writer, why did the soldiers at the back of the English army decide to run away? (2)
2. Look at **Source B**. Give two reasons why King Edward lost the battle. (3)
3. Look at **Source C**. With which source, **A** or **B**, does it most agree about why the English were unable to beat the Scots? Explain your answer. (7)
4. Look at **ALL** the sources. Which one do you think is the most useful evidence of what happened during the battle? (8)

**SOURCE A**: an extract from the *Lanercost Chronicle*, probably written in Carlisle soon after the battle.

When the two armies joined battle, the great English horses rushed on to the Scottish pikes, which bristled like a dense forest. An appalling din arose from the splintering pikes and the war-horses, mortally wounded. This brought matters to a standstill for a while. The English in the rear could not reach the Scots because their front line was in the way; indeed they could do nothing to improve their situation, and their only recourse was to fly. I heard tale of these events from a trustworthy eyewitness.

**SOURCE B**: an extract from *Military Blunders* by Geoffrey Regan, written in 1991.

Edward II had at his disposal overwhelming superiority in numbers and tactical options. Having brought a powerful English army into Scotland it was his dubious achievement to get it stranded in a position where it could not manoeuvre, leave his potentially 'battle-winning' archers underused at the rear, then to compound the folly [make the mistake worse] by quitting the field before the fight was over, causing the rest of his army to give up and flee.

**SOURCE C**: a 20th century painting of the battle, from the front cover of *Look and Learn* magazine (July 1965), showing the English knights unsuccessfully fighting against the Scottish pikemen.

# The Black Death 1348–1350

***Read the introduction and the sources and then answer all the questions. You must refer to the sources in ALL your answers.***

*The Black Death, or Bubonic Plague, was a disease that started in Asia. It spread westwards rapidly, reaching Europe in the 1340s and England by 1348. Between 1348 and 1350, about one third of England's population died of this mysterious and unseen enemy. The following sources give information about the symptoms and effects of this disease.*

1. Look at **Source A**. Give one reason why the families of plague victims had to bury their own dead. (2)
2. Look at **Source B**. Describe two kinds of plague symptoms mentioned by the writer. (3)
3. Look carefully at **Source C**. With which source, **A** or **B**, does it most agree concerning the plague? (7)
4. Look at **ALL** the sources. Which do you think gives the most useful evidence concerning the effects of the Black Death in England? (8)

**SOURCE A**: an extract from a 14th century writer describing the plague in Rochester.

Alas, this mortality [deathly disease] devoured such a multitude of both sexes, that no-one could be found to take the bodies of the dead to be buried. But men and women carried the bodies of their own little ones to church on their shoulders, and threw them into mass graves, from which arose such a stink that it was barely possible for anyone to go past a churchyard.

**SOURCE B**: an extract, from the modern historian M. Prestwich's book *Plantagenet England 1225–1360*, describing some of the symptoms of the Black Death.

Some victims had boils or abscesses. These broke out suddenly and when opened proved to be hard and dry. A good many survived this, either by cutting out the boils, or after a long period of illness. Others had small black spots full of puss all over their bodies. Hardly anyone survived from this form of the disease ... The most fatal form of the illness saw the patient cough up blood.

**SOURCE C**: a 14th century engraving of the Black Death.

# Henry V

***Read the introduction and the sources and then answer all the questions. You must refer to the sources in ALL your answers.***

*Henry V had many difficulties abroad. The French attacked English possessions in Gascony and Calais. Determined to reclaim his French lands, Henry invaded Normandy, seized Harfleur and marched on Calais. On the way, he encountered the French army at Agincourt. The following sources all provide evidence about this famous battle, fought on 25th October 1415.*

1. Look at **Source A**. Where did the first French attack come from? (2)
2. Look at **Source B**. According to the writer, what was the problem with the French leadership? (3)
3. Look at **Source C**. With which source, **A** or **B**, does it most agree about why the French attacks failed to defeat the English? Explain your answer. (7)
4. Look at **ALL** the sources. Which source do you think would be the least useful evidence as to what happened during the Battle of Agincourt? (8)

**SOURCE A**: an extract from a chronicle called *Gesta Henrici Quinti* ('The Deeds of Henry V'), written in 1416 by Thomas Elmham, one of Henry's priests who was at the battle.

Along the line were wedges of archers, who fixed stakes in front to stop cavalry attacks, as the King ordered … The French cavalry, positioned on their flanks, rushed against our archers, but quickly, God willing, they were forced to retreat because of the showers of arrows, except those who had impaled themselves on the stakes or had been killed.

**SOURCE B**: an extract about the battle from *Agincourt 1415* by Matthew Bennett and Jeffrey Burn, written in 1991.

Contemporaries are quite right in blaming the French for the carelessness that comes from over-confidence. The very same men who made a battle plan that could have defeated the English proved incapable of putting it into effect. The fault here lay once more with the lack of a single leader in the French camp. Experienced and important though they were, the Constable [d'Albret] and Marshall [Boucicaut], as the King's officers, could not outrank Princes of the Blood … once they were lumbered with a huge force and all the competing jealousies and arrogance of the French, they had no chance.

**SOURCE C**: a 20th century painting of the Battle of Agincourt by Peter Jackson, from *Treasure* magazine (April 1964).

# Women in Medieval Society

***Read the introduction and the sources and then answer all the questions. You must refer to the sources in ALL your answers.***

*During the Middle Ages, women played an important part in daily life. Their responsibilities were many and varied. What they did often depended upon whether they were rich or poor. The following sources give information about some of their numerous tasks.*

1. Look at **Source A**. Describe one task carried out by women when working with wool. (2)
2. Look at **Source B**. Give two skills which the writer says should be possessed by ladies managing their own landed estates. (3)
3. Look carefully at **Source C**. How far does it support Sources **A** and **B** concerning women's duties? (7)
4. Look at **ALL** the sources. Which do you think gives the most useful evidence concerning the duties of women in medieval society? (8)

**SOURCE A**: an extract, from the modern historian Jennifer Ward's book *Women in England in the Middle Ages*, describing some aspects of women's work.

Textiles provided employment for women in places where the industry flourished ... Women worked at washing and spinning wool. The wool had to be washed to get rid of the grease, and then carded [combed] before spinning. The spinner might be self-employed or work for a merchant. The wage in the mid-fifteenth century was generally 2d [about £4.00 today] for a pound of spun woollen yarn. Spinning brought work into the household, but a woman relying on spinning for her support would be poor.

**SOURCE B**: an extract from a 14th century book advising noble women about their duties concerning landed estates.

[Advice] for ladies living in castles or on their estates. These women spend much of their lives in households without husbands. The men usually are at court or in distant countries. So the ladies will have the responsibilities for managing their property. A woman must know the yearly income from her estate ... she should know how to manage accounts ... and in what season the fields should be fertilized ... and the best time for sowing. She must hire good labourers. She will insist that they get up early, [and] will rise early herself, put on a cloak, go to the window and watch there until she sees them go out, for labourers are usually inclined to laziness.

**SOURCE C**: a 14th century illustration of women spinning and carding wool.

# Evidence Questions

## B. The Making of the United Kingdom: 1485–1750

# Henry VII

***Read the introduction and the sources and then answer all the questions. You must refer to the sources in ALL your answers.***

*Henry VII rescued England from the chaos and disorder of civil war. Perhaps his greatest achievement was then to set his country upon the road to prosperity in a difficult age when new ideas mixed with old ways. As a man, Henry was cunning, suspicious and clever. He was also very fond of money and needed lots of it. The following sources all provide evidence about his reign (1485–1509).*

1. Look at **Source A**. According to the writer, was Henry a warlike king? (2)
2. Look at **Source B**. Give two reasons why Henry believed wealth to be so important for him as king. (3)
3. Look at **Source C**. In what ways does it support what Sources **A** and **B** say about Henry's attitude towards royal finance? (7)
4. Look at **ALL** the sources. Which one do you think would be the most useful to someone studying how important money was in Henry's reign? (8)

**SOURCE A**: an extract from Polydore Vergil's *Historia Anglica* ('History of England'), written on Henry VII's orders. It was finished in about 1535. Vergil had come to England in 1502, met Henry often and spoke to many people who worked closely with Henry.

He was distinguished, wise and prudent in character. In government he was shrewd … none got the better of him by deceit or sharp practice … by nature he preferred peace to war. Above all he cherished [valued] justice. In his later days, all these virtues were obscured by avarice [greed for money] … and in a monarch, it is the worst of all vices, since it hurts everyone, and distorts those qualities of trust, justice and integrity with which a kingdom should be governed.

**SOURCE B**: from the history book *Dictionary of History* by R. J. Unstead, published in 1976.

Realising that an impoverished [poor] king was weak, he amassed a fortune by various means, including forced 'loans' and heavy fines on those who displeased him. Wealth enabled him to overcome the nobles, since they were well aware that he could hire an efficient army to carry out his wishes. He also used his money and wits to advance the power and dignity of the Crown.

**SOURCE C**: a page of the royal accounts from Henry's reign. Henry has marked the entry with his initials, showing that he had checked it.

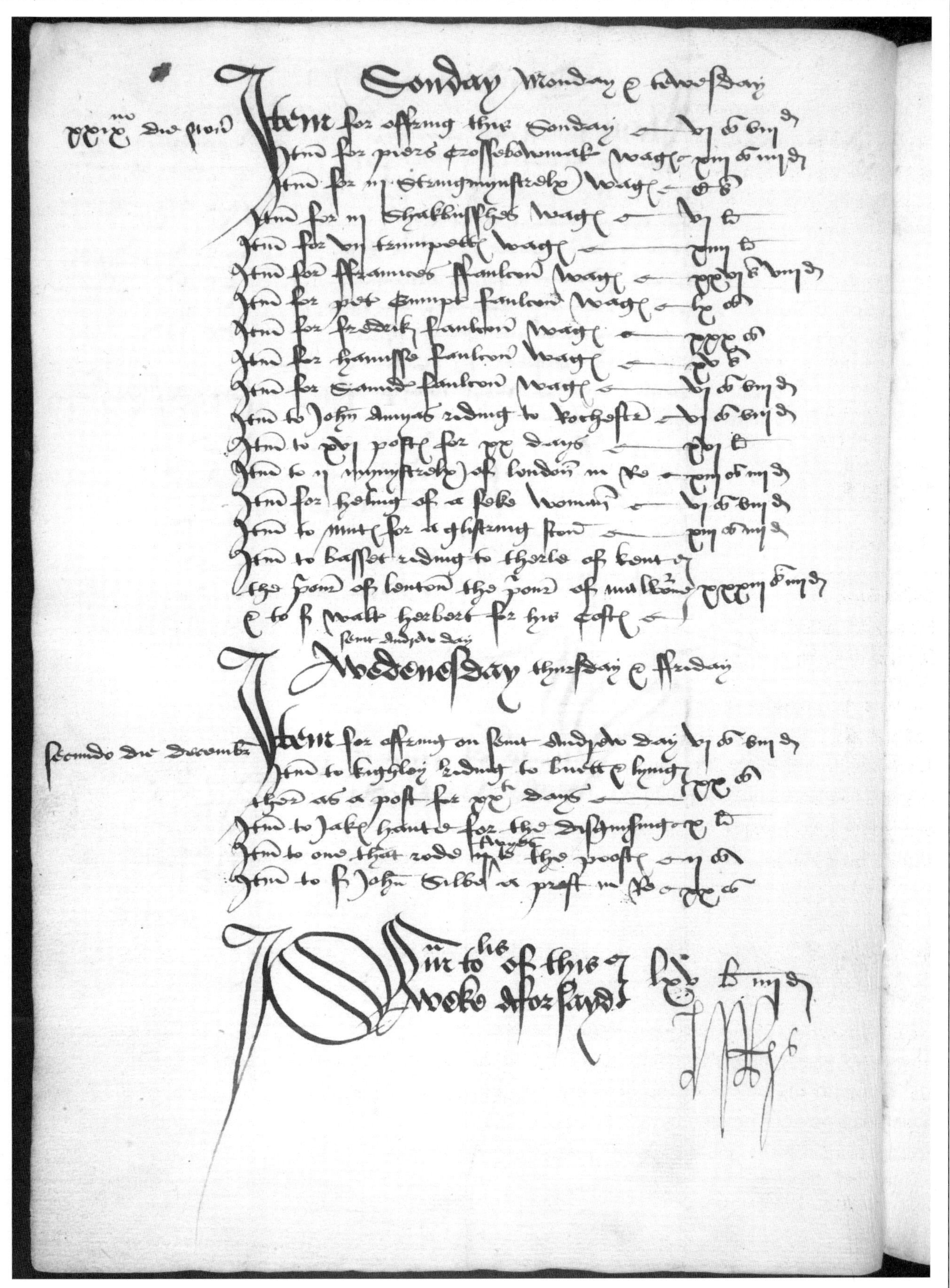

# Henry VIII

***Read the introduction and the sources and then answer all the questions. You must refer to the sources in ALL your answers.***

*Henry VIII enjoyed a triumphant journey through life. No king set out more determinedly to glorify the splendour and image of monarchy. He wanted fame, he relished greatness and presided over a spectacular court. He was the first English monarch to hold the title 'Defender of the Faith' and the first to adopt the practice of formally adding a number after his name. The following sources all provide evidence about his reign (1509–1547).*

1. Look at **Source A**. According to the writer, why was England so short of money by the end of Henry's rule? (2)
2. Look at **Source B**. Give two ways in which Henry could be seen as a king who had served his country well. (3)
3. Look at **Source C**. With which source, **A** or **B**, does it most agree about the success of Henry's reign? Explain your answer. (7)
4. Look at **ALL** the sources. Which one do you think would be the least useful to someone studying what Henry achieved as king? (8)

**SOURCE A**: an extract from the modern history textbook *The Early Modern Age* by L. E. Snellgrove.

Henry VIII had been cruel, selfish and arrogant. He had defied the pope, forced great changes on England and made the country bankrupt with his wars. He crushed both friends and enemies without pity. No man was a more typical 16th century ruler, caring little for individuals and behaving as God's representative on earth. The great square figure, legs apart, hands on hips, which stares at us from many of his portraits, casts a long shadow over English history.

**SOURCE B**: an extract from the modern history book *The Kings and Queens of England and Scotland* by Allen Andrew.

The achievements of Henry VIII's reign have often been obscured in the popular imagination by the story of his many marriages. It is overlooked that by 1547, when he died, England had broken with the power of the Roman Papacy, had become established as a rival of the European powers headed by the Emperor Charles V and Francis I of France, and laid the foundations for the golden age of Elizabeth I.

**SOURCE C**: The Whitehall Mural, by Hans Holbein, was produced around 1536. This is an engraving, after the painting, by George Vertue, called Familia Regia, or The Family of Henry VIII (1742). The writing on the tablet praises Henry VIII for being a greater king than his father, mainly as the 'power of the Pope bowed to his resolve [will]', as Henry VIII had broken with Rome.

# Henry VIII and his Great Matter

***Read the introduction and the sources and then answer all the questions. You must refer to the sources in ALL your answers.***

*The following sources give information about Henry VIII's 'Great Matter'. Henry VIII had received special permission from Julius II to marry Catherine of Aragon. Unable to persuade Clement VII to end the marriage, Henry had to take matters into his own hands.*

1. Look at **Source C**. Using the picture, describe how you think Catherine felt when she heard Cranmer's news. (2)
2. Look at **Source A**. Give two reasons why Henry VIII wanted to divorce Catherine. (3)
3. Look at **Source B**. In what ways does it support Sources **A** and **C**? (7)
4. Look at **ALL** the sources. Which do you think provides the most useful evidence for someone studying how Henry VIII obtained his divorce from Catherine? (8)

**SOURCE A**: an extract, from the 20th century textbook *The Early Modern Age* by L. E. Snellgrove, about Henry VIII's Divorce from Catherine of Aragon.

For some time Henry had been thinking of taking a new wife. He wanted a son to rule after his death; of Catherine's seven children, only a daughter, Mary, had lived. By 1527 it was obvious that the Queen was past child-bearing age ... This problem ... was made more urgent by the king's love for Anne Boleyn ... [Cranmer] was sent to the continent to consult foreign scholars about the problem ... Meanwhile Anne had at last given in to the king and was pregnant. In January 1533 the couple were secretly married ... later Cranmer held a court which declared that Catherine had never been Henry's wife in the eyes of the Church.

**SOURCE B**: an extract from Thomas Cranmer's *Sentence of Divorce*, 23rd May 1533.

In the name of God, Amen. We Thomas [Cranmer] ... Archbishop of Canterbury proceeding duly and legally ... concerning the validity of the marriage between the most illustrious and most mighty prince and lord, Henry VIII ... and the most high lady, Catherine ... having inspected the opinions of legal experts ... we separate and divorce them. And we pronounce [that] they are free ... from every bond of Matrimony [marriage].

**SOURCE C**: a 19th century French painting, by Eugene Deveria, showing Cranmer telling Catherine that she is to be divorced from Henry VIII.

# Lady Jane Grey and Mary I

***Read the introduction and the sources and then answer all the questions. You must refer to the sources in ALL your answers.***

*On 10th July 1553, it was announced that Jane Grey would be queen. Hearing this, Mary wrote to the Council demanding her right to the throne. She gathered her followers and marched on London. With Mary's support increasing, Jane Grey's father, the Duke of Suffolk, tore down the canopy of state hanging above her throne, telling his daughter that her short reign was over. The following sources all provide evidence about who would rule after Edward VI's death.*

1. Look at **Source A**. According to the writer, did people like the idea of Lady Jane Grey becoming Queen? (2)
2. Look at **Source B**. Give two ways Northumberland tried to stop Mary becoming Queen. (3)
3. Look at **Source C**. With which source, **A** or **B**, does it most agree about who was seen by people then as the rightful ruler of England after Edward's death? Explain your answer. (7)
4. Look at **ALL** the sources. How useful are they to someone studying the struggle to succeed Edward VI as ruler? (8)

**SOURCE A**: an extract from the Grey Friars chronicle, written at the time. It describes the reaction in London, first to the news of Lady Jane Grey becoming Queen, and then to Mary Tudor coming to the throne in 1553.

On the 10th of the same month, a proclamation was made, by heralds, with the King's Sheriff of London, that Jane, the Duke of Suffolk's daughter, would be the Queen of England, but few or none said 'God save her' … On the 19th of the same month, Lady Mary was proclaimed Queen of England, by the Earl of Shrewsbury, the Earl of Arundel, the Earl of Pembroke, the Mayor of London and the King's Sheriff [of London]. And the same night most parts of London celebrated with bonfires in every street, with good cheer everywhere, and the bells ringing in every parish church.

**SOURCE B**: from the modern history textbook *The Early Modern Age* by L. E. Snellgrove.

Northumberland decided on a wild scheme to save his skin. Edward was persuaded to make a will leaving the crown to the children of Lady Jane Grey, granddaughter of Henry VIII's sister. Henry had left the crown to Edward, then Mary and finally Elizabeth … When it became obvious that Edward would die before Lady Jane had a child, this will was altered to give the throne to Jane herself.

**SOURCE C**: a 20th century painting by John Byam Liston Shaw showing Mary being welcomed in London as Queen, with Princess Elizabeth standing behind her.

# Mary I and the Protestants

***Read the introduction and the sources and then answer all the questions. You must refer to the sources in ALL your answers.***

*The following sources give information about Mary I's treatment of Protestants. Thomas Cranmer was a Protestant Archbishop of Canterbury. He once signed documents renouncing Protestantism, but finally decided to return to it.*

1. Look at **Source A**. Describe one thing which Cranmer did at his execution. (2)
2. Look at **Source B**. Give two ways in which this source suggests that Cranmer had strong Protestant beliefs. (3)
3. Look at **Source C**. How far does it support Sources **A** and **B** in showing how Protestant martyrs died? (7)
4. Look at **ALL** the sources. Which do you think gives the most useful evidence concerning Mary's treatment of Protestants? (8)

**SOURCE A**: an extract, from the 20th century textbook *Thomas Cranmer* by D. MacCulloch, describing the death of Thomas Cranmer in March 1556.

The crowd arrived at the place where Latimer and Ridley had suffered six months before [16th October 1555]. Fire was put to wood. [Cranmer said] 'forasmuch as my hand offended, writing against the wishes of my heart, my hand shall be punished'. He stretched it out into the heart of the fire … he was very soon dead. It was said that in the ashes of the fire, his heart was found unburnt.

**SOURCE B**: an extract from John Foxe's *Book of Martyrs*, published in 1563 to glorify the Protestant Martyrs.

Then the Spanish friar, John, began to exhort him [press him to turn Catholic] but Cranmer bid him farewell … Then was an iron chain tied about Cranmer and when the wood was kindled and the fire began to burn near him … he put his right hand into the flame, which he held so steadfast and immoveable, that all men might see his hand burnt before his body was touched … his eyes were lifted up to heaven … he repeated the words 'Lord Jesus, receive my spirit' [and] in the greatness of the flames, he gave up the ghost.

**SOURCE C**: an 18th century engraving showing the burning of Protestant Martyrs in Smithfield, London.

# Elizabeth I

***Read the introduction and the sources and then answer all the questions. You must refer to the sources in ALL your answers.***

*Three weeks after becoming queen, Elizabeth was described by the Imperial Ambassador as 'A very strange sort of woman'. As a female in a largely male world, she devoted great attention to the presentation of her image. The following sources all provide evidence about the character of Queen Elizabeth I, who ruled from 1558 to 1603.*

1. Look at **Source A**. To what does the writer compare the effect of Elizabeth's bad moods? (2)
2. Look at **Source C**. Give examples that show the artist was more concerned with showing Elizabeth as an important ruler rather than how she actually looked. (3)
3. Look at **Source B**. In which ways does it agree with Sources **A** and **C**? Explain your answer. (7)
4. Look at **ALL** the sources. Which source would be least useful to someone studying Elizabeth's character? (8)

**SOURCE A**: a comment from Christopher Hatton, Elizabeth's Lord Chancellor, on what life at Court with her was like.

When she smiled it was pure sunshine that everyone did choose to bask in if they could, but bye and bye came a storm from a sudden gathering of the clouds, and the thunder fell in wondrous manner on all alike.

**SOURCE B**: an extract from *The Kings and Queens of England and Scotland* by Allen Andrew, published in 1976.

As queen, she was always ornately dressed with a profusion of jewels ... She was learned in six languages but had little taste for art or literature. Though she could assume majesty at any time, her language and her manners were coarse, and at Court she could still instil as much fear as her father had done.

**SOURCE C**: the 'Pelican Portrait' of Elizabeth by Nicholas Hilliard. It was painted around 1575 when she was 42, and was designed to show Elizabeth's love for her subjects as well as her royal power.

# The Causes of the Civil War 1629–1641

***Read the introduction and the sources and then answer all the questions. You must refer to the sources in ALL your answers.***

*An important cause of the Civil War occurred when the House of Commons, led by John Pym, turned against Charles I's two chief ministers, William Laud and the Earl of Strafford. In November 1640, they were sent to the Tower accused of treason. The following sources give information concerning the charges against Strafford and details of his final execution.*

1. Look at **Source A**. Why did Strafford's enemies decide to use a Bill of Attainder? (2)
2. Look at **Source B**. According to Pym, in what three main areas had Strafford's treason caused offence? (3)
3. Look carefully at **Source C**. How far does this source support the view implied in Sources **A** and **B** that Strafford was unpopular? (7)
4. Look at **ALL** the sources. Which do you think provides the least useful evidence as to why Strafford was executed? (8)

**SOURCE A**: an extract, from the modern textbook *The Early Modern Age* by L. E. Snellgrove, describing the trial of the Earl of Strafford.

Pym had to prove that Strafford was guilty of treason. Evidence was not easy to find ... After three weeks' trial there was still no verdict ... Strafford's enemies were now desperate. They therefore decided to switch to a Bill of Attainder which needed no proof but simply declared a person guilty of treason ... Charles promised Strafford he would save his life ... These rumours caused the London mob to riot ... Strafford was now sick and weary. He advised the king to let him die. Charles decided to sacrifice his minister.

**SOURCE B**: an extract from John Pym's charges against Strafford, made in November 1640.

These articles [charges] have expressed the character of a great and dangerous treason ... a treason against God, by betraying his truth and worship; against the king, by obscuring the glory and weakening the fundamental power of his throne; against the Commonwealth [England] by destroying the principles of safety and prosperity.

**SOURCE C**: a 17th century engraving showing the execution of the Earl of Strafford on Tower Hill, 12th May 1641.

# The Battle of Marston Moor

***Read the introduction and the sources and then answer all the questions. You must refer to the sources in ALL your answers.***

*Fought near York on 2nd July 1644, the battle of Marston Moor was a significant victory for the Parliamentary army under Cromwell, Fairfax and Manchester, over the Royalists, commanded by Prince Rupert. Following this defeat, the north of England was lost to the Royalist cause. The following sources all provide evidence about the battle.*

1. Look at **Source A**. Give one way you can tell which person is Oliver Cromwell. (2)
2. Look at **Source B**. According to the writer, why did God not favour either side? (3)
3. Look at **Source C**. With which source, **A** or **B**, does it most disagree about the battle? Explain your answer. (7)
4. Look at **ALL** the sources. Which source do you think provides the most useful evidence as to what happened during the Battle of Marston Moor? (8)

**SOURCE A**: an engraving by J. J. Crew, after Abraham Cooper, from a history book published in 1826, showing the wounded Oliver Cromwell leading the decisive final Parliamentarian charge.

**SOURCE B**: an extract from a letter by a royalist eyewitness to the battle, written soon afterwards.

More of the enemy were slain than of ours: more of ours taken [prisoner] than of theirs; but never were two such armies so suddenly and strangely scattered, and so few killed.

It was the hand of God on both parts: he seemed not to like their horrid rebellion nor our too much confidence. The truth is we had the victory but did not know it, and were content to give it to those that had not dared to come and fetch it [the Parliamentarians].

**SOURCE C**: an extract from the modern history book *British Battles* by Ken and Denise Guest, first published in 1996.

An unusually large number of casualties littered the moonlit landscape. Something approaching 6000 royalists had been slain or taken. The losses of the opposing side were lighter; from the jaws of defeat the Allied [Parliamentarian] army had snatched a most extraordinary victory.

# The Plague of London 1665

***Read the introduction and the sources and then answer all the questions. You must refer to the sources in ALL your answers.***

*The following sources give information about the London Plague of 1665. At its height, so many people were dying that many could not receive proper burials. It is reckoned that about half of London's population escaped into the country. Samuel Pepys, who lived and worked in London at the time, noted what he saw in his diary. Other people drew pictures showing scenes of the plague.*

1. Look at **Source A**. Give one reason why the bodies were not buried in the proper way. (2)
2. Look at **Source B**. Describe the three particular things which Pepys noted as he walked along. (3)
3. Look carefully at **Source C**. How far does this source support the information given in Sources **A** and **B**? (7)
4. Look at **ALL** the sources. Which do you think is the most useful to someone studying the history of the London Plague of 1665? (8)

**SOURCE A**: an extract, from the 20th century textbook *The Making of a Nation* by A. J. Patrick, about the Great Plague.

In the end, over a thousand people in the stricken city were dying of the plague each day. Life in the town came to a standstill. Those who could afford it left London … This meant that the streets, usually so busy, were still and quiet, disturbed only occasionally by the screams and groans of the sick and dying. So many died that there was no longer time or room to bury them properly. Instead of orderly funerals … the dead, like so much rubbish, were collected each night by a cart … The man in charge of it rang a hand-bell and shouted, 'Bring out your dead!'

**SOURCE B**: an extract from *The Diary of Samuel Pepys* describing what he saw in London at the time of the Plague.

I walked to the Tower. But, Lord, how empty the streets are, and sad. There are so many poor sick people in the streets, full of sores, and so many sad stories overheard as I walk. Everybody talking of this man dead, and that man sick, and so many in this place and so many in that.

**SOURCE C**: a 17th century woodcut showing plague bodies being buried.

# James II and the Glorious Revolution

***Read the introduction and the sources and then answer all the questions. You must refer to the sources in ALL your answers.***

*The following sources give information about the Glorious Revolution of 1688. James II had acted against the wishes of his people, so in 1688, a group of important men wrote to William of Orange asking him to come to rule England. James II fled to France.*

1. Look at **Source C**. Describe one sign of welcome to William. (2)
2. Look at **Source A**. Name two things which James II promised to respect. (3)
3. Look at **Source B**. How far does it support Sources **A** and **C** in showing most Englishmen's attitude to William? (7)
4. Look at **ALL** the sources. Which do you think gives the most useful evidence of why William III became King of England in 1688? (8)

**SOURCE A**: an extract, from the modern history book *The Revolution of 1688 in England* by J. R. Jones, explaining James II's intentions at the start of his reign in 1685.

James carefully ... stated his intention of respecting the religion, liberties and property of his subjects. He expressed his belief in the essential interdependence [working together] of the rights of the Crown with those of the people, and he was precise ... in the assurances which he gave to the Church of England.

**SOURCE B**: an extract from the Letter of Invitation asking William of Orange to become king, written in 1688.

The people are so generally dissatisfied with the present conduct of the government in relation to their religion, liberties and properties, and they are in such expectation of their prospects being daily worse, that your Highness may be assured there are nineteen parts of twenty of the people throughout the kingdom who are desirous of [want] change, and, we believe, would willingly contribute to it.

**SOURCE C**: an illustration from about 1850 showing William of Orange landing at Brixham, Devon on 5th November 1688.

# The Jacobite Rebellion of 1745

***Read the introduction and the sources and then answer all the questions. You must refer to the sources in ALL your answers.***

*The following sources give information about the Highland Charge. This was the special method of Jacobite attack used in the main battles of the 1745 Rebellion. It worked at Prestonpans and Falkirk, but failed at Culloden.*

1. Look at **Source A**. Give the main reason for Cope's defeat. (2)
2. Look at **Source B**. Describe the main stages of the Highland Charge. (3)
3. Look carefully at **Source C**. How far does this source support the information given in Sources **A and B**? (7)
4. Look at **ALL** the sources. Which do you think provides the most useful evidence as to what happened during the Highland Charge at the Battle of Prestonpans? (8)

**SOURCE A**: an extract, from the 20th century textbook *Bonnie Prince Charlie* by D. Daiches, describing the Highland Charge at the Battle of Prestonpans, 21st September 1745.

The reason for the speed and completeness of the defeat of Cope's army was partly ... the Highland method of attack. According to John Home [an observer at the time] the highlanders first fired on the dragoons, causing them to fall into confusion, then threw down their muskets, drew their swords and ran on.

**SOURCE B**: an extract from a Jacobite eyewitness account of Prestonpans written just after the battle.

The signal having been given to form up and attack, the Highlanders pulled off their bonnets, looked up to heaven, made a short prayer and ran forward. They received a very full fire, but advanced. They threw down their muskets and, drawing their broadswords, gave a most frightful and hideous shout, rushing most furiously upon the enemy, so that in seven or eight minutes, both horse and foot were totally routed and driven from the field of battle.

**SOURCE C**: a 19th century view of the Highland Charge at the Battle of Prestonpans.

# Evidence Questions

## C. Britain: 1750–circa 1900

# The French Revolution

***Read the introduction and the sources and then answer all the questions. You must refer to the sources in ALL your answers.***

*The French Revolution (1789) provoked a divided reaction in Britain. Many favoured early events like the storming of the Bastille or the abolition of feudalism. However, for some people, horror set in later as the blood began to flow and Louis XVI was guillotined in January 1793 by 'a legion of evil spirits'. The following sources all provide evidence about British feelings towards France after the French Revolution.*

1. Look at **Source A**. What proof does it give that some people in Britain had similar ideas to the reformers in France? (2)

2. Look at **Source B**. Give two reasons why the English gentleman in the story got so angry. (3)

3. Look at **Source C**. With which source, **A** or **B**, does it most disagree about how British people viewed the French Revolution? Explain your answer. (7)

4. Look at **ALL** the sources. Which source do you think provides the least useful evidence as to what people in Britain thought about the French Revolution? (8)

**SOURCE A**: an extract, from the modern history book *British History 1066–1900* by Walter Robson, about how people in Britain reacted to the French Revolution.

Men and women were shocked by the violence of the French Revolution. But some of them (called the 'radicals') were on the side of the French reformers. They thought that Britain also needed a good deal more freedom. They said that rule by king, lords, and gentry was unfair. By 1792 most towns in Britain had radical clubs.

**SOURCE B**: taken from the *Observer* newspaper, 1792.

Last night in a London coffee-house, a foreigner jumped up and started to make a speech. He called the King [of England] a tyrant and the people slaves. He said that in nine months' time the Jacobins of Paris [the revolutionary ruling party in France] would bring freedom to London. At this, an English gentleman seized him, gave him a horse-whipping, and kicked him out of the house.

**SOURCE C**: a pamphlet published in Britain in 1792, showing the writer's views of Britain and Revolutionary France.

# The Battle of Waterloo

***Read the introduction and the sources and then answer all the questions. You must refer to the sources in ALL your answers.***

*On Sunday, 18th June 1815, the French under Napoleon were defeated by an allied army commanded by Wellington and Blücher. On the order, 'prepare to meet cavalry', British infantry formed hollow squares three ranks deep, the outer ranks kneeling with the butts of their muskets resting on the ground, the bayonets pointing up and outwards. A steady square could not be taken by cavalry. The following sources give information concerning French cavalry attacks on British squares.*

1. Look at **Source A**. Give one reason why the French cavalry were unable to break the British squares. (2)

2. Look at **Source B**. Describe two results when the French cavalry attacked the British infantry. (3)

3. Look carefully at **Source C**. How far does it support the information given in Sources **A** and **B** concerning the French attacks on the British infantry squares? (7)

4. Look at **ALL** the sources. How useful are they to a historian trying to understand how British infantry dealt with French cavalry attacks at Waterloo? (8)

**SOURCE A**: an extract, from the modern historian D. Howarth's book *Waterloo: A Near Run Thing*, describing attacks by French cavalry at the Battle of Waterloo.

No-one could even remember afterwards how many times the cavalry came charging up the slope. Officially it was reckoned there were twelve attacks. Nor could anyone say how long it lasted: perhaps it was an hour and a half. In every charge, the same thing happened, the French cavalrymen found themselves vulnerable to musket shot [liable to be killed].

**SOURCE B**: a passage from *The Military Life of the Duke of Wellington* (author unknown), an English account of the Battle of Waterloo written in 1847.

Marshal Ney [commanding the left wing of Napoleon's army] was gathering his cavalry and soon forty squadrons stood ready to charge. Of these, more than half were the famous cuirassiers. Glittering in their steel breastplates and black, horse-hair crested helmets, they presented an unequalled display of gallant horsemen. Formed in a double line of squares, the British waited for the storm … The cuirassiers raised a loud cheer and dashed up to the faces of the squares. With the command to fire, the lines of leading horsemen fell or recoiled … Weakened by the fire and disordered, they retreated. Again and again were the charges repeated, but with equally fruitless results. At length, the broken squadrons retreated to their own positions.

**SOURCE C**: a 19th century painting showing Highlanders at Waterloo forming squares to withstand a cavalry charge from the French cuirassiers.

# The Great Reform Bill of 1832

***Read the introduction and the sources and then answer all the questions. You must refer to the sources in ALL your answers.***

*In June 1832 the Reform Bill became law, but only after a long struggle to steer it through Parliament. The House of Lords had protested against earlier versions of the Bill, which had led to unrest in some towns. Many who opposed reform feared that the passing of the Bill would cause a revolution. The following sources give information concerning Reform Bill riots.*

1. Look at **Source A.** Describe one thing which the rioters did. (2)
2. Look at **Source B.** Give two reasons why Macaulay thinks the 'lower orders' rioted in support of reform. (3)
3. Look carefully at **Source C**. How far does it support the information given in Sources **A** and **B** concerning Reform Bill riots? (7)
4. Look at **ALL** the sources. Which do you think provides the most useful evidence concerning the Reform Bill riots? (8)

**SOURCE A**: an extract, from the modern historian D. G. Wright's book *Democracy and Reform 1815–1885*, describing the Reform Bill Riots.

The London riots of [October] 1831 resulted in window smashing as well as assaults on Tory lords. Yet most of the rioters remained orderly ... Two days of rioting at Nottingham involved the setting fire to property and a factory. But no lives were lost ... In Derby there were three days of rioting [and] although troops arrived and quickly restored order, three bystanders were killed. Most serious of all were the Bristol riots. For two days Bristol was in the hands of the rioters. Public buildings ... were attacked and destroyed. Twelve men were killed and over a hundred wounded.

**SOURCE B**: an extract from a speech in Parliament by Thomas Babington Macaulay in March 1831. Macaulay was a young man who supported the cause of reform.

Unhappily, the lower orders in England are occasionally in a state of great distress [poverty and suffering] ... we know what effect distress produces, we know that it makes even wise men irritable and unreasonable, eager for immediate relief; that it [distress] blunts their judgement, that it inflames their passions. I support this measure because I am sure it is our best security against a revolution. I support this measure as a measure of reform, but I support it still more as a way of preserving ourselves [the middle and upper classes].

**SOURCE C**: a 19th century engraving, from *Cassell's Illustrated History of England* (1895), showing Queen's Square, Bristol during Reform Bill riots on the night of 30th October 1831.

# Chartism

***Read the introduction and the sources and then answer all the questions. You must refer to the sources in ALL your answers.***

*The Chartists were a group of working-class political reformers seeking the vote for all men. They were so named because they presented their ideas in the form of a six-point Charter. This Charter, along with petitions requesting various social and economic improvements, was submitted to Parliament in 1839, 1842 and 1848. It was rejected. The following sources give information concerning the introduction of the Charter to the House of Commons.*

1. Look at **Source A.** Give one reason why it may be said that Parliament did not favour the Chartists. (2)
2. Look at **Source B.** Describe two methods used by Thomas Attwood when trying to champion the Chartists' cause. (3)
3. Look carefully at **Source C**. With which other Source, **A** or **B**, does it most agree concerning the extent of Chartist support throughout the country? (7)
4. Look at **ALL** the sources. Which do you think makes the most useful contribution to our understanding of Chartism? (8)

**SOURCE A**: an extract, from the modern historian N. McCord's book *British History, 1815–1906*, describing the Chartists' use of the petition and Parliament's reaction to it.

One of the repeatedly employed methods of Chartism was the great national petition. Repeated use of this device was itself an indication that the movement lacked any means of putting effective pressure on the state ... There can be no doubt that the Chartist petitions contained the genuine signatures of hundreds of thousands of people. But the authorities never intended to yield to their demands. Instead, the House of Commons refused even to consider the mass Chartist petitions. For example, the first great petition was denied a hearing in 1839 by 235 votes to 46.

**SOURCE B**: an extract from a speech by Thomas Attwood introducing the Charter and the First Petition to Parliament on 14th June 1839. Attwood was a great supporter of the Chartists.

[He said] the Petition originated in the town of Birmingham ... it was forwarded to Glasgow where it received the signatures of 90,000 honest men. I hold in my hand a list of two hundred and fourteen towns and villages in different parts of Great Britain where the Petition has been adopted and signed ... and it is now presented with 1,280,000 signatures. The men who signed the Petition were honest and industrious, men of sober and unblemished character, men who have discharged the duties of good members of society and who have always obeyed the laws.

**SOURCE C**: a 19th century engraving showing Thomas Duncombe presenting the Second Petition to Parliament in May 1842. This Petition contained over three million signatures.

# The Crimean War

***Read the introduction and the sources and then answer all the questions. You must refer to the sources in ALL your answers.***

*Keen to prevent any Tsarist expansion into Europe at Turkish expense, which might threaten her political and economic power, Britain fought against the Russians in the Crimean War (1854–1856). The following sources all provide evidence about the Charge of the Light Brigade, which took place on 25th October 1854, during the battle of Balaclava.*

1. Look at **Source A**. According to the writer, how many men took part in the charge? (2)
2. Look at **Source B**. What types of fire did Lieutenant Phillips face as he charged? (3)
3. Look at **Source C**. With which source, **A** or **B**, does it most disagree about the detail of the charge? (7)
4. Look at **ALL** the sources. Which one do you think would be the most useful evidence as to what happened to the Light Brigade? (8)

**SOURCE A**: a verse from Alfred Lord Tennyson's poem *The Charge of the Light Brigade*, written in 1854 in response to the reported British heroism in the charge.

Cannon to the right of them,
Cannon to the left of them,
Cannon in front of them
Volley'd and thunder'd
Storm'd at with shot and shell,
Boldly they rode and well,
Into the jaws of Death,
Into the mouth of Hell
Rode the six hundred.

**SOURCE B**: an extract from an account written by Lieutenant Edward Phillips, who took part in the charge.

We advanced at a steady trot, soon to a faster pace; we had not advanced 200 yards before the guns [artillery] on our left and right opened fire; two regiments of infantry drawn up on our right began firing volleys and almost at the same time the guns at the bottom of the valley opened up. In spite of this awful fire, we galloped over the ground strewed with men of the first line, and our own dropping every yard.

**SOURCE C**: a painting from 1855 by William Simpson showing the charge by the 673 men of the Light Brigade. He did not see it, but he visited the battlefield several weeks later, and showed his sketches to the Earl of Cardigan who had led the charge. However, to make the scene more dramatic, he made the valley much smaller and showed the regiments much too close together.

# The Indian Mutiny

***Read the introduction and the sources and then answer all the questions. You must refer to the sources in ALL your answers.***

*On 10th May 1857, Indian troops in the British Army (sepoys) shot their officers and mutinied. Other Sepoy regiments of the North-West provinces followed suit. For a time it seemed as though the whole of British power in India would crumble. The English settlement at Cawnpore was besieged and its European inhabitants were massacred. The British eventually restored order, but there was horror and brutality on both sides. The following sources give information concerning some of the cruelties of the uprising.*

1. Look at **Source A**. Describe how the men were killed. (2)
2. Look at **Source B**. Give two reasons why the Cawnpore garrison surrendered to the rebels. (3)
3. Look carefully at **Source C**. How far does it support Sources **A** and **B**? (7)
4. Look at **ALL** the sources. Which do you think offers the most useful evidence to someone studying the cruelties of the Indian Mutiny? (8)

**SOURCE A**: an extract from a British account of the Cawnpore Massacres written in 1857.

The women and children were dispatched [killed] first with swords and spears. The men were arranged in line, with a bamboo running along the whole extent and passing through each man's arms, which were tied at the back. The [Indian] troops then rode about them and taunted their victims. One of them would discharge [fire] a pistol in the face of a captive, whose shattered head would drop to the right or left ... not a soul escaped.

**SOURCE B**: an extract, from the modern historian Sir L. Woodward's book *The Age of Reform 1815–1870*, describing the massacres of the British at Cawnpore in the summer of 1857.

Cawnpore was surrounded by mutineers. Three hundred British officers and men ... and four hundred women and children were crowded into the fortified camp. The garrison was attacked by 3,000 sepoys ... Food supplies were running short, and there seemed no chance that reinforcements would arrive before they were starved out ... Wheeler [the garrison commander] accepted the offer of safe conduct [but] the men were killed and the women and children who survived the sabres of the mutineers were imprisoned. [When a British force approached] the rebel leader ordered his troops to kill all the women and children in his prison ... Five men hacked the prisoners to death with knives and threw the bodies into a well.

**SOURCE C**: a 19th century British painting, from *The History of the Indian Mutiny* (1858), showing rebel sepoys being blown to bits at the mouth of British guns.

# The Cotton Industry

***Read the introduction and the sources and then answer all the questions. You must refer to the sources in ALL your answers.***

*Spinning was a skilled craft and the machinery used became increasingly complicated to operate. Nonetheless, children were widely used in cotton mills. They were cheap to employ and worked long hours, performing a variety of factory tasks for low wages. They laboured with little hope of promotion. The following sources give information concerning the part played by children in cotton mills.*

1. Look at **Source A**. Give one reason why children came to be employed to perform minor tasks in cotton mills. (2)
2. Look at **Source B**. Describe the jobs of two members of a team operating a spinning mule. (3)
3. Look carefully at **Source C**. How far does it agree with the information provided in Sources **A** and **B**? (7)
4. Look at **ALL** the sources. Which do you think offers the most useful evidence concerning the part played by children in cotton mills? (8)

**SOURCE A**: an extract, from the modern historian P. Kirby's book *Child Labour in Britain 1750–1870*, describing the use made of children in early factories.

Early factories did contain large concentrations of child workers and offered new opportunities for children to work, [but] as spinning machines became more complicated, their direct operation was unsuitable for young children. Instead, children were employed in tasks secondary to the main process of production.

**SOURCE B**: an extract from a late-18th century description explaining how a team of workers operated a mule [a machine for spinning].

In working the common mule various persons are employed. The *spinner,* who directs the general operation of the machine, one or more *piecers,* to join the threads which break during the spinning … and a *cleaner* or *scavenger,* to remove waste cotton and to clean the machine generally. The spinner in most cases [is] an adult; the others being subordinate [junior] to him are always young persons or children.

**SOURCE C**: a 19th century engraving showing adults operating spinning mules while a child crawls under the moving machine to sweep up.

# Trade Unions

***Read the introduction and the sources and then answer all the questions. You must refer to the sources in ALL your answers.***

*After 1815, with high post-war unemployment, increasing urban and rural unrest, and famine never very far away, some men banded themselves into unions. Their aim was to improve pay and conditions. Although unions became legal in 1824, such activities generated government alarm. Repression often followed. The following sources all provide evidence about the early struggles facing workers who tried to form trade unions.*

1. Look at **Source A**. According to the writer, why did Loveless want to form a branch of the GNCTU? (2)
2. Look at **Source B**. How did the opponents of trade unions try to get rid of them? (3)
3. Look at **Source C**. How does it agree with the information given in Sources **A** and **B**? (7)
4. Look at **ALL** the sources. Which one do you think would be the most useful evidence about the problems that the early trade unions faced? (8)

**SOURCE A**: an extract from a modern history textbook by Peter Lane.

A Tolpuddle labourer, George Loveless, sent for officials of the GNCTU [the union founded by Robert Owen] to help form a branch of the union when, in 1833, farm workers' wages were lowered … In February 1843 the magistrates … warning against the forming of a union branch … arrested Loveless and the five other leaders.

The sentence imposed was seven years' imprisonment in Tasmania … and Melbourne, as Home Secretary, congratulated the magistrates.

**SOURCE B**: an extract from the modern history book *British History 1066–1900* by Walter Robson.

Employers did not like the unions. Some used lock-outs to try to smash them. (They closed their works, and gave the men their jobs back only if they left the union.) And the government took the employers' side.

Robert Owen tried to set up a union for all trades and for the whole of England in 1834. But it lasted only for a few months … News of the Tolpuddle Martyrs killed Owen's union. Workers did not want to risk transportation for themselves and ruin for their families.

**SOURCE C**: the notice posted by Dorset magistrates in 1834, stating what would happen to Loveless and his followers if they formed a union.

# CAUTION.

**WHEREAS it has been represented to us from several quarters, that mischievous and designing Persons have been for some time past, endeavouring to induce, and have induced, many Labourers in various Parishes in this County, to attend Meetings, and to enter into Illegal Societies or Unions, to which they bind themselves by unlawful oaths, administered secretly by Persons concealed, who artfully deceive the ignorant and unwary,—WE, the undersigned Justices think it our duty to give this PUBLIC NOTICE and CAUTION, that all Persons may know the danger they incur by entering into such Societies.**

ANY PERSON who shall become a Member of such a Society, or take any Oath, or assent to any Test or Declaration not authorized by Law—

Any Person who shall administer, or be present at, or consenting to the administering or taking any Unlawful Oath, or who shall cause such Oath to be administered, although not actually present at the time—

Any Person who shall not reveal or discover any Illegal Oath which may have been administered, or any Illegal Act done or to be done—

Any Person who shall induce, or endeavour to persuade any other Person to become a Member of such Societies,

WILL BECOME

## Guilty of Felony,

AND BE LIABLE TO BE

## Transported for Seven Years.

ANY PERSON who shall be compelled to take such an Oath, unless he shall declare the same within four days, together with the whole of what he shall know touching the same, will be liable to the same Penalty.

Any Person who shall directly or indirectly maintain correspondence or intercourse with such Society, will be deemed Guilty of an Unlawful Combination and Confederacy, and on Conviction before one Justice, on the Oath of one Witness, be liable to a Penalty of TWENTY POUNDS, or to be committed to the Common Gaol or House of Correction, for THREE CALENDAR MONTHS; or if proceeded against by Indictment, may be CONVICTED OF FELONY, and be TRANSPORTED FOR SEVEN YEARS.

Any Person who shall knowingly permit any Meeting of any such Society to be held in any House, Building, or other Place, shall for the first offence be liable to the Penalty of FIVE POUNDS; and for every other offence committed after Conviction, be deemed Guilty of such Unlawful Combination and Confederacy, and on Conviction before one Justice, on the Oath of one Witness, be liable to a Penalty of TWENTY POUNDS, or to Commitment to the Common Gaol or House of Correction, FOR THREE CALENDAR MONTHS; or if proceeded against by Indictment may be

## CONVICTED OF FELONY,

## *And Transported for SEVEN YEARS.*

*COUNTY OF DORSET,*
*Dorchester Division.*

February 22d, 1834.

C. B. WOLLASTON,
JAMES FRAMPTON,
WILLIAM ENGLAND,
THOS. DADE,
JNO. MORTON COLSON,

HENRY FRAMPTON,
RICHD. TUCKER STEWARD,
WILLIAM R. CHURCHILL,
AUGUSTUS FOSTER.

# Slavery and the Triangular Trade

***Read the introduction and the sources and then answer all the questions. You must refer to the sources in ALL your answers.***

*Throughout the 18th century, thousands of black Africans from West Africa were taken in British ships to work as slaves in the Americas. This was part of the so-called Triangular Trade. British ships took goods to Africa, then took African slaves to America, finally sailing back home with goods produced by slave labour. The following sources give information about the conditions on slave ships.*

1. Look at **Source A**. Give one reason why the traders packed as many slaves as possible into a slave ship. (2)
2. Look at **Source B**. From this evidence, describe two ways in which slaves might suffer at sea in such conditions. (3)
3. Look carefully at **Source C**. How does it help us to understand the information given in Sources **A** and **B** concerning the situation of slaves on slave ships? (7)
4. Look at **ALL** the sources. Which do you think makes the most useful contribution to our understanding of the conditions in which slaves were shipped to the Americas? (8)

**SOURCE A**: an extract, from the modern historian A. M. Newth's book *Britain and the World, 1789–1901*, describing the conditions on board a slave ship.

The worst horror was perhaps the 'middle passage' as the voyage to America was called. The slaves were packed as tightly as possible because, as the traders argued, even if many of them did die, it was worth the risk, for the profit they would make for each one they landed was enormous.

**SOURCE B**: an 18th century slave-trader describes life on a slave ship.

She [the slave ship] had taken in 336 males and 226 females on the coast of Africa, making in all 562, and had been out [at sea] seventeen days, during which she had thrown overboard 55. The slaves were all enclosed under grated hatchways between decks. The space was so low that they sat between each other's legs and were stowed [packed in] so close together that there was no possibility of their lying down or at all changing their positions night or day. The circumstance [fact] which struck us most forcibly was, how it was possible for such a large number of human beings to exist packed up and wedged together as tight as they could cram … the greater part of which were shut out from light or air.

**SOURCE C**: an 18th century engraving showing the stowing of slaves in a British slave ship.

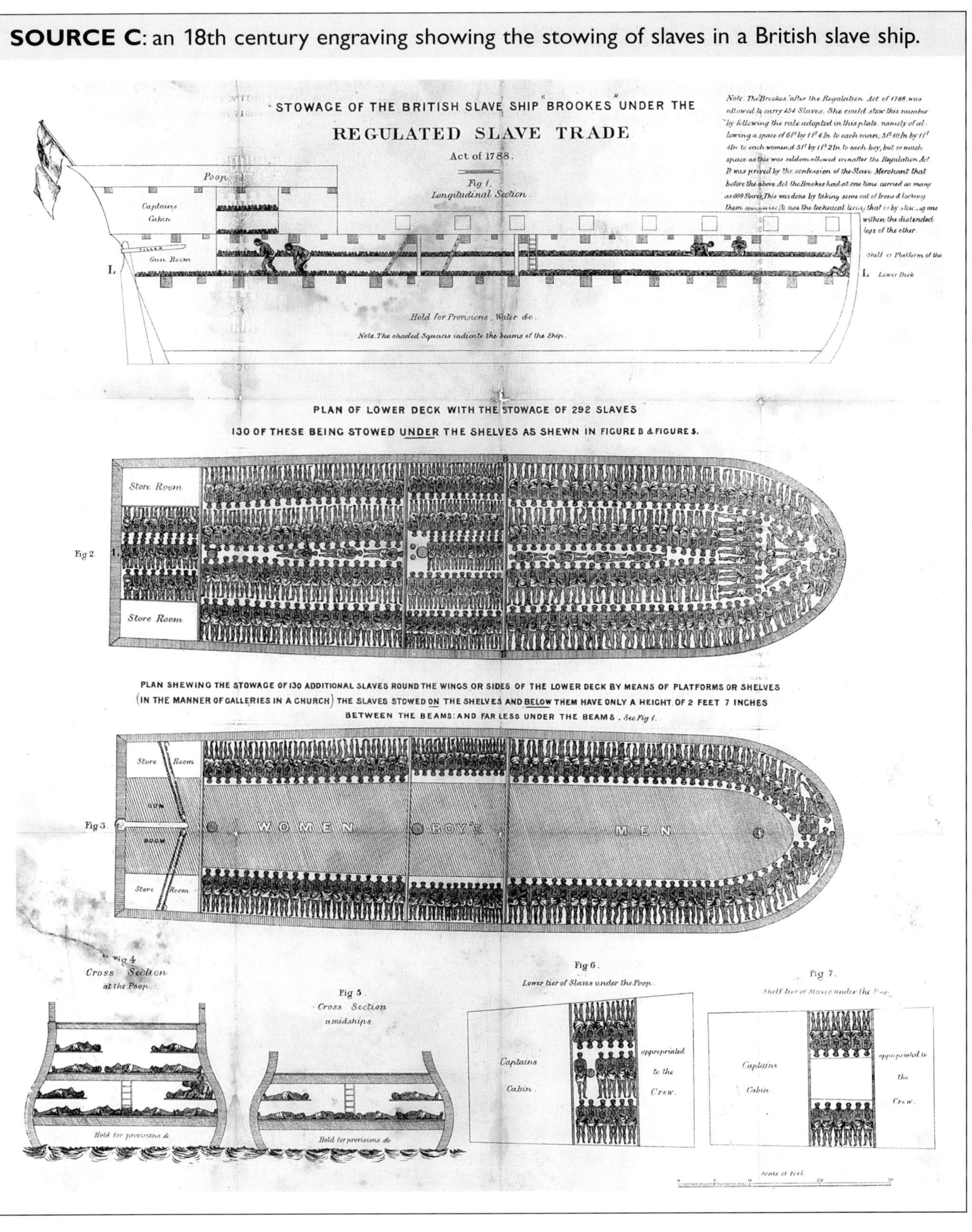

# The British Empire

***Read the introduction and the sources and then answer all the questions. You must refer to the sources in ALL your answers.***

*From the early 17th century, Britain built up a huge empire. At its peak, around 1920, it was said to comprise one quarter of the world's land area and to contain a fifth of its population. It was claimed that 'the sun never set' on British possessions. The following sources all provide evidence about British attitudes to their Empire.*

1. Look at **Source A**. According to the writer, how did Egyptians respond to the British and French interfering in their country? (2)
2. Look at **Source B**. Give two reasons why the British Empire came about. (3)
3. Look at **Source C**. With which source, **A** or **B**, does it most agree about how British people viewed their Empire? Explain your answer. (7)
4. Look at **ALL** the sources. Which source do you think would be the least useful evidence as to the importance of the British Empire to people at the time? (8)

**SOURCE A**: an extract from a meeting of the Workmen's Peace Association on 24th June 1882, responding to the crisis following anti-British riots in Egypt, which was then largely ruled by Britain.

At a time when people are demanding that our forces should attack Egypt, we have to ask the reason why. A few years ago, our government and the French began to interfere in Egypt, without having any right to do so. The result was that the National Party [of Egypt] was formed. Its slogan was 'Egypt for the Egyptians'. If Englishmen cried 'England for the English' we would praise them. So why should we condemn Egyptians for doing the same?

**SOURCE B**: an extract from *Understanding History 2* by John Child et al, a modern history book.

One reason for the creation of the British Empire was trade … But there were other reasons. The government sometimes took over areas for their strategic value. Some British missionaries also thought they were 'civilising' the native peoples. At first the British public were not much interested in the idea of an empire. It wasn't until about 1870 that imperialism – enthusiasm for empire – became common among ordinary people in Britain.

**SOURCE C**: a cartoon from *Punch* magazine (1882), showing Great Britain (the lion) as being the rightful leading imperial power in Egypt and Africa.

THE LION'S JUST SHARE

# Essay Questions

## A. Medieval Realms: Britain 1066–1485

## War and Rebellion

1. (a) Describe the main events of the Battle of Hastings. (20)

   (b) Explain how William I gained control over his new kingdom. (10)

2. (a) Describe the key details of the civil war between Stephen and Matilda. (20)

   (b) Explain the main causes of this civil war. (10)

3. (a) Describe the main events of Edward I's campaigns against the Welsh. (20)

   (b) Explain what Edward I did to keep control of the Welsh. (10)

4. (a) Describe the main events of the Battle of Bannockburn. (20)

   (b) Explain how the result of this battle affected Edward II's position as king. (10)

5. (a) Describe the main features of the Battle of Crécy. (20)

   (b) Explain the effects of this battle on the development of the war against France up to 1360. (10)

6. (a) Describe the main stages of the Battle of Agincourt. (20)

   (b) Explain why Henry V was able to be victorious in the battle. (10)

7. (a) Describe the part played by Joan of Arc in the war against Henry VI. (20)

   (b) Explain how the events of the war against France affected Henry VI's position as King of England. (10)

8. (a) Describe the main details of the Wars of the Roses between 1455 and 1485. (20)

   (b) Explain the causes of this conflict. (10)

## Government and Parliament

1. (a) Describe the means by which medieval kings between 1066 and 1215 tried to extend control over their realms. (20)

   (b) Explain the main factors which determined the success or failure of their various attempts. (10)

2. (a) Describe the main elements of the baronial revolts against King John. (20)

   (b) Explain the importance of Magna Carta. (10)

3. (a) Describe the main events of the Peasants' Revolt. (20)

   (b) Explain why the revolt occurred. (10)

4. (a) Describe the main features of the Model Parliament of 1295. (20)

   (b) Explain how far this event was important in the development of Parliament. (10)

5. (a) Describe the struggles between Henry II and Thomas Becket. (20)

   (b) Explain the effects of Becket's murder on Henry II. (10)

## Religion

1. (a) Describe the ideal routines of daily life inside a medieval monastery. (20)

   (b) Explain why monasteries had become so powerful by 1500. (10)

2. (a) Describe the events of the church career of John Wycliffe. (20)

   (b) Explain why he is seen as such an important figure of the medieval Church. (10)

3. (a) Describe the main events of the Third Crusade. (20)

   (b) Explain whether or not you believe this crusade was a success. (10)

4. (a) Describe the usual duties of a hard-working village priest in medieval England. (20)

   (b) Explain why a good priest was so important to a village community during the Middle Ages. (10)

## Social History

1. (a) Describe the main details of the development of the Black Death in England from 1348 to 1349. (20)

   (b) Explain the effects of the Black Death on life in the countryside. (10)

2. (a) Describe the key features of peasant life in a medieval village. (20)

   (b) Explain how a lord of the manor ran his village. (10)

## General Topics

1. (a) Describe the part played by women in medieval life. (20)

   (b) Explain why women were not seen as being equal to men in medieval times. (10)

2. (a) Describe the main developments in the style of castle building from 1066 to around 1500. (20)

   (b) Explain why medieval castles were built in particular places. (10)

3. (a) Describe the key features of the career of Simon de Montfort. (20)

   (b) Explain why he may be regarded by historians as a failure or a success. (10)

4. (a) Describe the main features of the career and work of the poet, Geoffrey Chaucer. (20)

   (b) Explain why he should be regarded as an important medieval writer. (10)

5. (a) Describe some of the main details of the Bayeux Tapestry. (20)

   (b) Explain why it is such an important piece of evidence for historians. (10)

# Essay Questions

## B. The Making of the United Kingdom: 1485–1750

## War and Rebellion

1. (a) Describe how Henry VII gained the crown in 1485. (20)

   (b) Explain why he was victorious at the Battle of Bosworth. (10)

2. (a) Describe the main events of the Pilgrimage of Grace. (20)

   (b) Explain why this rebellion failed. (10)

3. (a) Describe the main details of Kett's Rebellion and the Prayer Book Rising of 1549. (20)

   (b) Explain why the rebels were unsuccessful. (10)

4. (a) Describe the important features of the Lady Jane Grey Plot. (20)

   (b) Explain the main effects of this plot on the monarchy. (10)

5. (a) Describe the career of Mary Queen of Scots after her arrival in England. (20)

   (b) Explain the ways in which Mary was dangerous to Elizabeth I. (10)

6. (a) Describe the main events of the war with Spain 1588–1603. (20)

   (b) Explain how the results of this war affected England. (10)

7. (a) Describe the main reasons why the Duke of Monmouth rebelled in 1685. (20)

   (b) Explain how much of a threat this rebellion was to the government of the time. (10)

8. (a) Describe the main events of the Jacobite Rebellion of 1745. (20)

   (b) Explain why Charles Stuart failed to overthrow George II. (10)

## Government and Parliament

1. (a) Describe the main events of Henry VII's work as king in England. (20)

   (b) Explain how Henry VII's policies served to make England strong. (10)

2. (a) Describe the main features of Thomas Wolsey's career. (20)

   (b) Explain why he fell from power. (10)

3. (a) Describe the main events of Thomas Cromwell's career in government. (20)

   (b) Explain what you think was his greatest achievement. (10)

4. (a) Describe the work of William Cecil (Lord Burghley) in his time as the chief minister of Elizabeth I. (20)

   (b) Explain how successful Cecil was in running the government for Elizabeth I. (10)

5. (a) Describe the main quarrels between Elizabeth I and her Parliaments. (20)

   (b) Explain how successful Elizabeth was in managing Parliament. (10)

6. (a) Describe the relations between James I and Charles I and their Parliaments in the period from 1603 to 1642. (20)

   (b) Explain how the actions of James I and Charles I affected the history of England in this period. (10)

7. (a) Describe the main features of Oliver Cromwell's period of power from 1649 to 1658. (20)

   (b) Explain how far you think Cromwell was a success. (10)

8. (a) Describe the main developments in the relationship between the Crown and Parliament in the period 1660–1688. (20)

   (b) Explain how the power of Parliament changed during this time. (10)

9. (a) Describe the main reasons for the passing of the Act of Union (1707). (20)

   (b) Explain how the passing of this Act affected the history of the United Kingdom. (10)

10. (a) Describe the main achievements of Sir Robert Walpole. (20)

    (b) Explain why he fell from power in 1742. (10)

## Religion

1. (a) Describe the main features of the Church in England before the Reformation. (20)

   (b) Explain why the condition of the Church led many people to seek religious change. (10)

2. (a) Describe the main stages of Henry VIII's reformation of the Church. (20)

   (b) Explain why Henry was able to change the Church so quickly. (10)

3. (a) Describe the most important religious changes which occurred in the reign of Edward VI. (20)

   (b) Explain how Edward's changes affected the future of religion up to 1558. (10)

4. (a) Describe the main features of the Elizabethan Church Settlement of 1559. (20)

   (b) Explain why Elizabeth wanted to make such a settlement. (10)

5. (a) Describe the position of Puritans and Roman Catholics during the reign of Elizabeth I. (20)

   (b) Explain how Puritans and Roman Catholics tried to improve their religious position within England. (10)

6. (a) Describe the main features of Archbishop Laud's religious policies. (20)

   (b) Explain how successful you believe Laud was in achieving his goals. (10)

7. (a) Describe the religious opinions and influences of the Puritans between 1603 and 1649. (20)

   (b) Explain the most important consequences of their beliefs. (10)

8. (a) Describe how and why John Bunyan was persecuted. (20)

   (b) Explain whether Bunyan was strengthened or weakened by this persecution. (10)

## Social History

1. (a) Describe the enclosure movement of the 16th century. (20)

   (b) Explain the effects of enclosure on both the rich and the poor of the time. (10)

2. (a) Describe the main features of the wool trade in the 16th century. (20)

   (b) Explain how the trade in wool benefited England during this time. (10)

3. (a) Describe the main features of overseas trade in the period 1500–1750. (20)

   (b) Explain how and why the governments of the time tried to encourage the development of overseas trade. (10)

4. (a) Describe the main details of life at Court in the reign of Charles I. (20)

   (b) Explain how some features of Court life might have led people to oppose Charles I in 1642. (10)

5. (a) Describe the main details of the Elizabethan Poor Law system. (20)

   (b) Explain why Elizabeth I's Poor Laws are important. (10)

6. (a) Describe the main features of life in the countryside during the first half of the 18th century. (20)

   (b) Explain how and why country life was changing during this period. (10)

## General Topics

1. (a) Describe the main features of the lives of women in the period from about 1700 to 1750. (20)

   (b) Explain the importance of women in this period. (10)

2. (a) Describe the main details of the rise of Louis XIV's power in Europe between about 1660 and 1702. (20)

   (b) Explain how this affected the history of England at this time. (10)

3. (a) Describe the main achievements of the architect, Christopher Wren. (20)

   (b) Explain why you think it is important for historians to study the history of buildings and architectural design. (10)

4. (a) Describe the career of Sir Isaac Newton. (20)

   (b) Explain what you consider to be Newton's greatest achievement. (10)

5. (a) Describe the main events of the Great Fire of London in 1666. (20)

   (b) Explain what was done to try to stop the blaze. (10)

# Essay Questions

## C. Britain: 1750–circa 1900

## War and Rebellion

1. (a) Describe the main events of the Seven Years' War. (20)

   (b) Explain why the result of this war was of great benefit to England. (10)

2. (a) Describe the circumstances leading to the outbreak of the American War of Independence in 1776. (20)

   (b) Explain how the results of this war affected England's position in the world. (10)

3. (a) Describe the major causes of the French Revolution in 1789. (20)

   (b) Explain why the French revolutionaries were able to chop off Louis XVI's head in 1793. (10)

4. (a) Describe the main details of the Battle of Trafalgar. (20)

   (b) Explain what effect Nelson's victory had on the future conduct of the war against France. (10)

5. (a) Describe the main events of the Crimean War (1854–1856). (20)

   (b) Explain why England's leaders considered that it was important to enter this war. (10)

6. (a) Describe the key events of the Indian Mutiny of 1857. (20)

   (b) Explain why the mutiny broke out. (10)

7. (a) Describe the main events of the Boer War (1899–1902). (20)

   (b) Explain the consequences of this war for Britain. (10)

8. (a) Describe the career of the Duke of Wellington in the war against France. (20)

   (b) Explain the importance of what you consider to be his most famous victory. (10)

## Government and Parliament

1. (a) Describe the main details of the 1832 Reform Bill. (20)

   (b) Explain why this act was thought to be necessary. (10)

2. (a) Describe the most important political beliefs of the Chartists. (20)

   (b) Explain how far you think that the Chartists were successful in achieving their aims. (10)

3. (a) Describe the career of the political thinker, Jeremy Bentham. (20)

   (b) Explain Bentham's importance as a political reformer. (10)

4. (a) Describe the main events of Robert Peel's career as Prime Minister (1841–1846). (20)

   (b) Explain what you consider to have been his greatest political achievement. (10)

## Religion and Social Reform

1. (a) Describe the development of Methodism and its main features in this period. (20)

   (b) Explain how successful the Methodist movement had become by 1900. (10)

2. (a) Describe the main details of the Roman Catholic Emancipation Act of 1829. (20)

   (b) Explain how this Act came into being and why it was considered necessary. (10)

3. (a) Describe the work of Elizabeth Fry as a prison reformer. (20)

   (b) Explain the reasons for the beginning of the movement to reform prisons. (10)

## Social and Economic History

1. (a) Describe the main developments of the Agricultural Revolution. (20)

   (b) Explain the good and bad effects of agricultural change on different groups of people within England. (10)

2. (a) Describe the benefits of the development of railways during the Industrial Revolution. (20)

   (b) Explain why the revolution in steam transport did not help everyone in Britain. (10)

3. (a) Describe the main developments in textile manufacturing during the Industrial Revolution. (20)

   (b) Explain why the Industrial Revolution first took place in Britain. (10)

4. (a) Describe the most important achievements of Isambard Kingdom Brunel. (20)

   (b) Explain Brunel's importance to the industrial development of Britain. (10)

5. (a) Describe the main stages in the development of the police force within this period. (20)

   (b) Explain why it was important for Britain to improve its methods of enforcing law and order during the 19th century. (10)

6. (a) Describe the background to the trial of the Tolpuddle Martyrs in 1834. (20)

   (b) Explain the importance of the Tolpuddle case for the working-class movement of the time. (10)

7. (a) Describe the most important events in the development of trade unions up to 1901. (20)

   (b) Explain how trade unions tried to improve workers' lives. (10)

## General Topics

1. (a) Describe what was on offer for visitors to see at the Great Exhibition of 1851. (20)

   (b) Explain the importance of the Exhibition for Britain. (10)

2. (a) Describe the main stages in the development of the British Empire in this period. (20)

   (b) Explain the ways in which Britain benefited from imperial expansion. (10)

3. (a) Describe the most important achievements of Florence Nightingale. (20)

   (b) Explain what impact she had on British society. (10)

4. (a) Describe the main features of the career of Charles Darwin. (20)

   (b) Explain the importance of Darwin both in his own time and in today's world. (10)

5. (a) Describe the most important points in the career of Charles Dickens. (20)

   (b) Explain how he made an impact on his own times. (10)

6. (a) Describe the main details of the Unification of Germany (1862–1871). (20)

   (b) Explain how German unification affected Britain. (10)

7. (a) Describe the causes, details and effects of the Irish potato famine between 1845 and 1851. (20)

   (b) Explain the impact of this famine on Anglo-Irish relations in the second half of the 19th century. (10)